THE SCIENCE BEHIND
NATURAL
DISASTERS

EARTHQUAKES

THE SCIENCE BEHIND SEISMIC SHOCKS AND TSUNAMIS

Dr. Alvin Silverstein, Virginia Silverstein,
and Laura Silverstein Nunn

Enslow Publishers, Inc.
40 Industrial Road
Box 398
Berkeley Heights, NJ 07922
USA

http://www.enslow.com

Library of Congress Cataloging-in-Publication Data:

Silverstein, Alvin.
    Earthquakes : the science behind seismic shocks and tsunamis / Dr. Alvin
Silverstein, Virginia Silverstein, and Laura Silverstein Nunn.
        p. cm. — (The science behind natural disasters-)
    Includes bibliographical references and index.
    Summary: "Examines the science behind earthquakes and tsunamis, includ-
ing what makes them happen, where they occur, how they are measured, and
tips to stay safe during an earthquake"—Provided by publisher.
    ISBN-13: 978-0-7660-2975-0
    ISBN-10: 0-7660-2975-1
    1. Earthquakes—Juvenile literature. 2. Tsunamis—Juvenile literature.
I. Silverstein, Virginia B. II. Nunn, Laura Silverstein. III. Title.
    QE521.3.S5378 2010
    551.22–dc22
                        2008038589

Printed in the United States of America

10 9 8 7 6 5 4 3 2 1

To Our Readers:
We have done our best to make sure all Internet Addresses in this book were
active and appropriate when we went to press. However, the author and the
publisher have no control over and assume no liability for the material avail-
able on those Internet sites or on other Web sites they may link to. Any com-
ments or suggestions can be sent by e-mail to comments@enslow.com or to
the address on the back cover.

♻ Enslow Publishers, Inc., is committed to printing our books on recycled
paper. The paper in every book contains 10% to 30% post-consumer waste
(PCW). The cover board on the outside of each book contains 100% PCW.
Our goal is to do our part to help young people and the environment too!

Illustration Credits: AP/Wide World Photos, pp. 1, 4, 6, 30; Chen Yuxiao/
ChinaFotoPress/ Getty Images, p. 16; D. Parker/ Photo Researchers, p. 8;
David Parker/ Photo Researchers, Inc., p. 36; Enslow Publishers, Inc., p. 34;
Gary Hincks/ Photo Researchers, Inc., pp. 11, 13, 18, 20, 21; Jes Aznar/ AFP/
Getty Images, p. 27; Jianan Yu/ Reuters/ Landov, p. 22; Reuters/ Nicky Loh/
Landov, p. 26; Shutterstock Images, p. 10, 41.

Cover Illustration: Jianan Yu/ Reuters/ Landov

CONTENTS

WORLD SERIES
EARTHQUAKE

On October 17, 1989,

the third game of the World Series was about to start at Candlestick Park. It was a battle between two California baseball teams, the Oakland Athletics and the San Francisco Giants. During the fourth inning, the television signal broke up. Sportscaster Al Michaels yelled out, "I'll tell you what—we're having an earth—," and TV screens around the country went blank.[1] Minutes later the TV network switched to a telephone connection. Al Michaels explained that there was a power outage due to an earthquake.

Oakland Athletics pitcher Storm Davis helps a woman with a baby in the stands during an earthquake that struck during Game 3 of the World Series in San Francisco on October 17, 1989.

When the earthquake hit, the stadium rumbled with tremendous force. The shaking lasted only fifteen seconds, but to those inside it seemed *much* longer. No one was hurt inside Candlestick Park, but everyone had to leave.

The World Series Earthquake is officially known as the Loma Prieta Earthquake. Loma Prieta is a mountain in northern California, located in the Santa Cruz Mountains. The earthquake

Workers check the damage to Interstate 880 in Oakland, California, on October 19, 1989. The freeway collapsed after a major earthquake hit the Bay area.

caused serious damage as far as 97 kilometers (60 miles) away. The earthquake completely destroyed many houses. In San Francisco and Oakland, huge cracks split through sidewalks and roadways.

More than forty people died when the Cypress Bridge on Interstate 880 in Oakland collapsed.[2] A huge section of the San Francisco–Oakland Bay Bridge broke off as well. The earthquake set off many landslides and rockfalls. One major highway was blocked so badly that it had to be closed to traffic for a month.

All together, the Loma Prieta Earthquake killed 63 people and injured 3,757.[3]

Was Loma Prieta the "Big One?"

Scientists say "No." The deadliest earthquake in American history was the Great San Francisco earthquake of 1906. It had an estimated magnitude of 7.8. (A quake higher than magnitude 7 is a major earthquake.) Much of the city was destroyed, not because of the earthquake itself but because of the huge fires that broke out. At least 3,000 people died in this disaster, and about 225,000 were left homeless.[4]

Since the Great San Francisco earthquake of 1906, scientists have been saying that the next "big one" would hit California within the next hundred years or so. The Loma Prieta earthquake of 1989 was not powerful enough to be the "big one." It had a magnitude of only 6.9, less than the 1906 quake.

UNDERSTANDING EARTHQUAKES

What makes the earth shake?

And why are earthquakes more common in certain places? The answer lies deep below Earth's surface.

Earth's Layers

Our planet is made up of layers. The outer layer is the crust. It is solid rock. The crust is thickest under the continents and much thinner under the oceans.

The middle layer is the mantle. It makes up about 80 percent of the Earth's volume. The mantle is very hot. Temperatures range from 700° C (1300° F) to over 4,000° C (7,200° F). At the outer surface of the mantle, just under the crust, rocks actually melt. The melting rocks form a liquid called magma. The magma

The San Andreas Fault extends almost the full length of California and is responsible for major earthquakes. This desert landscape consists of pressure ridges formed as a result of hundreds of fault movements.

Picture This...

Think of the earth as layered, like a giant piece of fruit. Its core is like the pit of a cherry or peach. The mantle is like the layer of juicy pulp in the middle of the fruit. The crust is like the outer skin of the fruit. Compared to the size of the whole Earth, the crust is a very thin "skin."

is under high pressure from the heavy weight of the crust above it.

The deepest layer is the core, at the center of the earth. Scientists believe the earth's core is made up of molten metal, mainly iron. It is extremely hot there—more than 5,000° C (9,000° F)!

Moving Parts

Earth's rocky crust is not one big solid ball. The crust, together with a layer of hard mantle just beneath it, is broken up into about thirty pieces. These pieces are called tectonic plates. The plates fit together like the pieces of a jigsaw puzzle. They float on a hot layer of mantle. Sometimes the floating plates pull apart, push into each other, or slide along each other in different directions.

The edges of tectonic plates are called plate boundaries. When the plates move, their movement puts stress on the

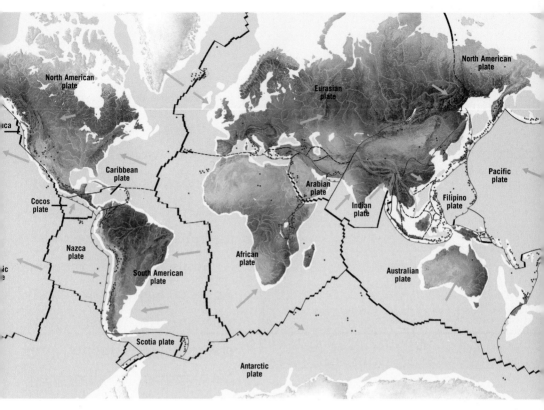

The Earth's surface is divided up into tectonic plates. The pink arrows show the direction that the plates move.

rocks near plate boundaries. Stress builds up and causes faults (cracks) in Earth's crust. Most earthquakes occur in the fault regions at plate boundaries. Eventually,

> *** It's a Fact! ***
> Earth's tectonic plates move very slowly—from one to ten centimeters (a half an inch to four inches) per year. This is the same rate fingernails grow!

the rock breaks under the stress, and the ground at the surface shakes. This ground-shaking is called a tremor.

Most faults develop deep in Earth's crust. But some can actually be seen on the surface. One famous example is the San Andreas

Why Do Tectonic Plates Get Locked Together?

When tectonic plates rub against each other, they produce friction. This is a force that works against movement. For example, friction stops a moving car when the driver presses on the brake. Friction between tectonic plates can lock them together.

Fault, which runs two-thirds of the length of California. (This fault was involved in the 1989 World Series Earthquake and in the Great San Francisco earthquake of 1906 as well.)

Some parts of the San Andreas Fault move slowly and steadily. These slow, creeping movements produce frequent small or moderate earthquakes. In other parts of the fault, pieces of the plates get locked together and cannot slide as the plates move. Stresses build up on both sides of the fault for tens or hundreds of years and then produce devastating earthquakes. (The buildup and sudden release of stress is very much like what happens when you stretch a rubber band until it breaks.) The same thing happens at other faults around the world.

Scientists describe three main types of plate boundaries:

Divergent boundaries. At these boundaries, magma rises to the surface. The plates pull apart, like two giant conveyer belts moving in opposite directions. As the hot molten rock cools, it hardens to form new crust at their edges. The Mid-Atlantic Ridge is the best-known example of this type.

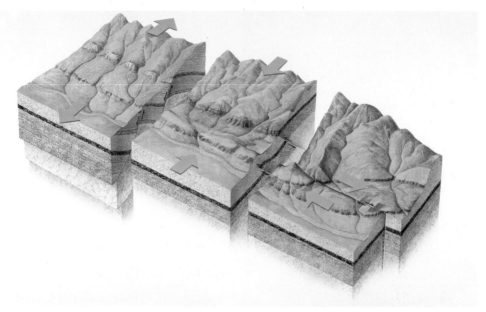

A fault produced by stretching is called a normal fault (left). A fault produced when the crust is pushed together is called a reverse fault (center). A fault where the two pieces of crust slide against each other is called a strike-slip fault (right). If the stress on a fault causes sudden breaking, the masses of rock on either side can move rapidly, producing an earthquake.

Convergent boundaries. Plates move toward each other at convergent boundaries. When two plates collide, one may slip underneath the edge of the other and sink into the mantle. This process is called subduction. Eventually (over millions of years), magma melts the plate. The amount of crust destroyed at convergent boundaries is about the same as the new crust being formed at divergent boundaries.

The subducted plate creates a very deep, narrow trench at the boundary. Subduction may also produce active underwater volcanoes. The huge trench that runs along the Pacific Ocean is

Can Earthquakes and Volcanic Eruptions Occur Together?

Yes. Earthquakes typically occur just before and during volcanic activity. Such earthquakes are usually rather minor. Mount Saint Helens in Washington erupted in May 1980. In the weeks before the massive eruption, thousands of minor earthquakes shook the mountain. Even as late as 2008, Mount Saint Helens had a series of small eruptions and earthquakes.

nicknamed the "Ring of Fire" because earthquakes and volcanoes are very common there.

When two continental plates come together, they push into each other head-on. As they collide, their edges buckle upward or sideways, forming mountains, such as the Himalayas.

Transform boundaries. At transform boundaries, plates slide past each other. No crust is destroyed and no new crust is formed. Most transform boundaries are under the oceans, but a few are found on continents. For example, California's San Andreas Fault is a transform boundary.

Earthquake Belts

Earthquakes are most common in three main "earthquake belts" in different parts of the world.

About 81 percent of the world's largest earthquakes occur along the Ring of Fire.[1] This earthquake belt is shaped like a horseshoe and curves around the Pacific Ocean.

The second main earthquake zone, known as the Alpide belt, has 17 percent of the world's largest earthquakes.[2] This belt stretches from Indonesia across to Greece and Turkey.

The third main zone lies along the Mid-Atlantic Ridge. This underwater mountain range runs north-south through most of the Atlantic Ocean.

Other earthquakes are scattered in various parts of the world. In these areas, earthquakes occur along faults that are far away from plate boundaries. In the United States, a famous example is the New Madrid Fault in the middle of the North American plate.

No matter where an earthquake occurs, it can cause a lot of destruction. For this reason, scientists have studied what happens when the ground starts shaking.

WHEN THE EARTH SHAKES

When fans "do the wave"

at a baseball game, their arms look like an ocean wave moving through the crowd. Scientists say the energy that produces earthquakes also moves in waves. But these waves are far more powerful than any ordinary ocean wave. They can cause solid rock to move and break. Earthquake waves can cause a lot of damage because of their tremendous force.

On Shaky Ground

What happens during an earthquake? Stresses build up underground around fault lines. Rock can handle a certain amount of stress, but eventually it breaks or slips into a new position. This

People flee a landslide on a speed boat as a result of aftershocks on May 19, 2008, in Yingxiu, Sichuan Province, China. A week after a major earthquake, fears of aftershocks caused thousands of people to camp in the streets instead of staying in their homes.

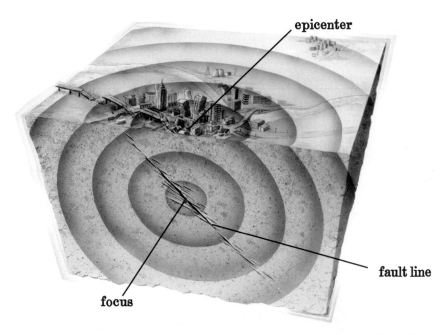

epicenter

fault line

focus

Earthquakes happen along a fault line. The place where the earthquake originates is the focus. The point on the surface directly above the focus is the epicenter.

movement releases stored-up energy and sets off vibrations in Earth's crust.

The place where the rock edges of plates break or move is called the focus of the earthquake. The focus is usually deep underground—from dozens to hundreds of kilometers (miles) below the surface. The spot on the surface directly above the focus is called the epicenter of the earthquake. It is here that the most severe damage usually occurs. The vibrations, called seismic waves, spread out from the focus in all directions.

Seismic waves come in two main forms: body waves and surface waves. Body waves move through the earth's inner layers. Surface waves travel only through the Earth's outermost layers—

the crust and the upper part of the mantle.

Body waves. These are the first seismic waves to arrive during an earthquake. There are two types of body waves: primary waves (P waves) and secondary waves (S waves).

P waves are the fastest. Speeding along at 24,135 kilometers (15,000 miles) per hour, P waves move through solid rock, air, and liquids,

Animals and Earthquakes

It was once thought that animals could sense when an earthquake is coming. Dogs have barked wildly for no obvious reason. Ducks and geese have left their ponds. Some scientists say this proves that animals can sense earthquakes before they happen. Other scientists, including those at the U.S. Geographical Survey, think that animals act strangely for other reasons and cannot predict earthquakes.

such as water and magma. The waves push and pull the rock, like the movement in a Slinky toy.

S waves are the second type of seismic wave to arrive. S waves are slower than P waves. They can move only through solid materials, at a speed of about 14,481 kilometers (9,000 miles) per hour. They make side-to-side or up-and-down movements, like ocean waves.

As the body waves travel underground, away from the focus, the P waves cause the rocks to be pushed and pulled. Buildings rocked by these waves shake up and down because the waves are arriving from below. Then come the S waves, which cause rocks and buildings to move from side to side.

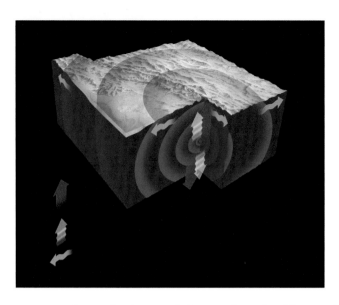

The waves move out from the focus of the earthquake. The earthquake causes P waves (red), S waves (yellow), and surface waves (lavender).

Surface waves. These waves are the last to arrive. Usually they cause the most damage during an earthquake. If the earthquake is deep underground, however, surface waves will have little effect. There are two types of surface waves: Love waves and Rayleigh waves.

Love waves are faster. They move the ground from side to side as they travel through the earth's surface.

Rayleigh waves move more slowly. They roll along the earth's surface like waves on the ocean. As they roll along, the Rayleigh waves move the ground up and down and side to side.

Before the main earthquake, sometimes there are one or more rather small earthquakes, called foreshocks. After the main earthquake, there are often additional, small quakes, called aftershocks. They may occur for days, weeks, months, or even years afterward. Generally, after-shocks are weaker than the main earthquake. But some-times, if the aftershock is close to a heavily populated area, it may cause more damage than the main quake. Aftershocks usually occur because only part of the stress built up in the rocks was released by the main earthquake.

How Long Do Earthquakes Last?

Most earthquakes last for less than fifteen seconds, but rare ones may go on for a minute or more. The longest-lasting earthquake ever recorded was about ten minutes. It occurred on December 26, 2004, off the coast of Indonesia, and caused huge deadly ocean waves (tsunamis).[1]

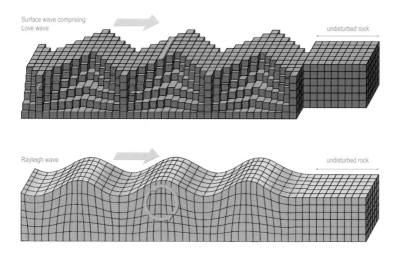

The Love wave (top) causes the ground to move (blue arrows) at right angles to the direction of the wave's movement (yellow arrow). Rayleigh waves (bottom) are similar to waves in water, in which the ground moves in a rolling manner. Surface waves are usually responsible for much of the damage that occurs in an earthquake.

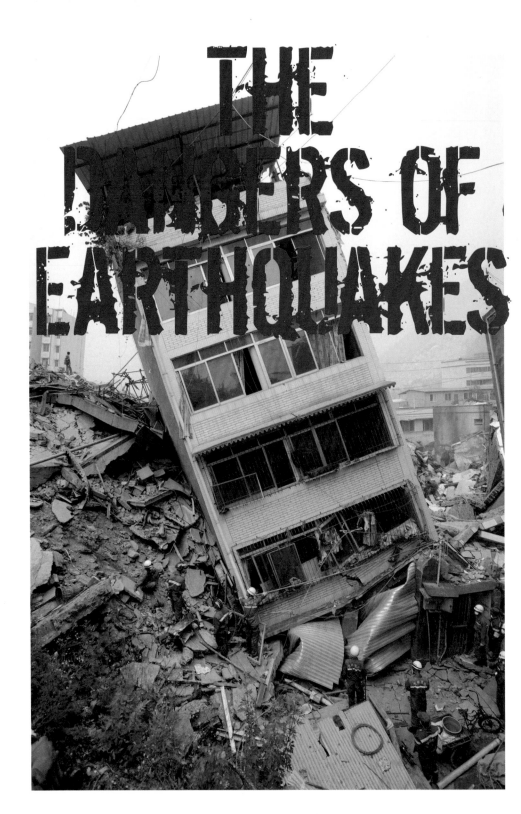

THE DANGERS OF EARTHQUAKES

Every year, scientists detect

roughly five hundred thousand earthquakes worldwide. Many of them go unnoticed because they are very weak. An estimated one hundred thousand quakes can be felt, but only about one hundred are strong enough to cause damage.[1]

Many earthquakes occur in areas where very few people live. With few buildings, even a strong earthquake will not cause much damage. But if an earthquake hits a big city, such as San Francisco, it can cost billions of dollars in damages. It can also be very dangerous to people and animals.

Rescuers search for survivors around a building in Beichuan, in China's Sichuan province, on May 17, 2008, after a massive earthquake in southwestern China.

Shake, Rattle, and Flow

In an earthquake, the ground shakes violently. The breaking rock along the earth's surface may form huge cracks in the ground and through sidewalks and roadways. Powerful surface waves make buildings, houses, and bridges sway. This motion can cause these structures to crack and break apart. In major earthquakes, buildings may even crumble to the ground.

Liquefaction occurs when the tremors mix sand or soil with water underground. The ground can then act like quicksand during the earthquake. Liquefaction can cause buildings to lean, tip over, or sink a meter or so (more than 3 feet). It can also cause serious damage to bridges.

Falling Objects

During an earthquake, falling objects can be very dangerous. In a house or apartment, strong tremors can tip over bookcases and other heavy furniture. Objects can fall from ceilings and shelves. Walking outside can be dangerous, as well. Traffic lights and street signs may suddenly topple over. Power lines may come down. Bricks from a building may fall down to the street below.

In many earthquakes, falling debris (pieces) from damaged buildings cause most of the deaths and injuries.

Raging Fires

An earthquake can start fires by breaking gas lines and power lines, or tipping over wood or coal stoves. If the water lines are broken, too, firefighters will have trouble keeping the fires from spreading. In just a short amount of time, these fires can easily sweep through whole neighborhoods. (Remember that fires burned down much of the city during the 1906 San Francisco earthquake.)

Can Earthquakes Be Predicted?

Not really. Instruments that record seismic waves are set up in areas with frequent earthquakes. However, scientists cannot tell exactly where and when an earthquake will happen. They have been unable to predict many earthquakes, and they have forecast quakes that never happened.

Foreshocks are not reliable warnings, either. They may occur days, months, or even years before a major earthquake. And many earthquakes have no foreshocks.

Landslides and Avalanches

Earthquakes can shake rocks loose from the sides of mountains. These rocks may crash down the mountain in landslides. Landslides can block highways, damage buildings, and kill people.

A man walks past fallen rocks on a road in the earthquake-hit town of Beichuan, in China's Sichuan province, on May 18, 2008.

Earthquakes can also trigger avalanches on snow-covered mountains. Avalanches have buried whole towns in snow.

Measuring Earthquakes

Earthquakes occur every day somewhere within the earth. Many thousands of earthquakes are detected each year. However, most quakes are so faint that even the best instruments do not detect them.

Scientists known as seismologists detect, measure, and study earthquakes, using instruments called seismographs. Seismographs work by measuring the movement of the ground and how fast the seismic waves are moving. Some seismographs can detect the seismic waves that form when rocks move beneath the earth, even ones that have formed thousands of miles away. Others contain devices called tiltmeters. These instruments can detect tiny earth movements that may signal an oncoming earthquake. When seismic

Scientist Jane Punongbayan points to the seismograph readings of the 6.0-magnitude earthquake that shook the city of Manila in the Philippines on November 27, 2007.

The First Seismograph

A Chinese scientist, Chang Heng, invented an instrument for detecting earthquakes back in A.D. 132. A pendulum in the center was attached to a ring of eight dragon heads, each of which held a bronze ball in its mouth. Eight statues of toads with open mouths sat directly below the dragons. If an earthquake occurred, the first tremors set the pendulum swinging. Then a ball dropped from one of the dragons into the mouth of the toad beneath it. The toad that caught the ball indicated the direction of the earthquake.

waves are detected, a seismograph produces wavy lines that are recorded on computers.

Two different scales are used to measure earthquakes: the Richter scale and the Mercalli scale.

The Richter magnitude scale gives a number rating showing the earthquake's power or "magnitude." The higher the number, the bigger the earthquake. An earthquake with a magnitude up to 2 can be detected only by instruments. At a Richter magnitude of 3 to 4, hanging lights sway and there may be minor damage. At magnitude 5 to 6, dishes, books, or other objects may fall off their shelves, and walls of buildings may crack. An earthquake with a magnitude of 7 or greater is considered major. It can make buildings collapse and cause highways and bridges to buckle and twist. No earthquake with a magnitude greater than 10 has ever been detected.

The Modified Mercalli Intensity scale is based on an earthquake's effects, rather than its power. It applies only to populated areas. Seismologists use observations rather than instruments to make an intensity rating.

The Mercalli scale has a 12-point rating scale. The higher the number, the higher the intensity. For example, a rating of 2 points indicates a barely noticeable earthquake. An earthquake with a Mercalli intensity of 10 points causes major damage to buildings, bridges, and other structures. An earthquake has different effects in different areas. So there are always different intensity values measured from one earthquake.

Mercalli scores are not as scientific as Richter magnitudes. They are based on people's descriptions and ratings of damage, rather than waves recorded on a seismograph. Also, the amount of damage depends on the distance from the epicenter, the structures of the buildings, and the kind of material they rest on. A building resting on solid rock, for example, usually will not shake as much as one built on sand.

Earthquakes that occur on the ocean floor do not damage buildings or kill people directly. However, they can cause huge waves, called tsunamis, that sweep over nearby coastal lands. The flooding produced by tsunamis can devastate local communities.

TSUNAMIS

One of the world's most powerful

earthquakes was an underwater earthquake. It happened on December 26, 2004, deep in the Indian Ocean off the west coast of Indonesia. The earthquake had a magnitude of 9.1 to 9.3. The powerful movements of the ocean floor created a tsunami that flooded entire communities. Indonesia, Sri Lanka, India, and Thailand were among the hardest hit regions. Some reports estimated more than 280,000 deaths—most of them caused by the tsunami that followed the earthquake![1]

A British family vacationing at a resort at Patong Beach in Phuket, Thailand, took this video image of the giant wave coming ashore on December 26, 2004. The video of the tsunami, sparked by an earthquake off the coast of Indonesia's Sumatra island, was filmed from the balcony of the family's hotel. Notice that the small building at the left of the photo is completely destroyed.

What Is a Tsunami?

A tsunami is a large, destructive ocean wave, caused mainly by an earthquake or volcanic eruption. Tsunamis are most common in the Pacific Ocean around the Ring of Fire. They have also occurred in other bodies of water, including the Caribbean and Mediterranean seas, and the Indian and Atlantic oceans.

Most tsunamis are caused by earthquakes on the ocean floor. But underwater volcanoes and landslides can also cause tsunamis. Even a meteorite from outer space falling into the ocean can cause tsunamis, although this is rare.

* It's a Fact! *

Tsunami is a Japanese word meaning "harbor wave." Japan has had at least fifteen devastating tsunamis in the past three hundred years. Japan is located in an especially active earthquake region because it lies where four tectonic plates meet.

How Do Tsunamis Form?

During an underwater earthquake, the ocean floor shifts, causing it to rise or drop. This movement can cause the ocean waters to rise. The waters start to move away from where the ocean plates shifted. The effect is something like tossing a rock into a pond. A circle of ripples forms where the rock went into the water and moves outward.

In the deep ocean water, a tsunami moves really fast. It can travel as fast as a jet airplane—about 805 kilometers (500 miles) per hour. It can also cover great distances. The 2004 Indian Ocean tsunami actually traveled throughout the world's oceans. It registered on seismographs as far away as South Africa and even Iceland.

Tsunami waves do not rise very high in the deep water. They may be only 61–91 centimeters (2–3 feet) high. A ship could pass right over a tsunami and not notice it at all.

As the tsunami moves to shallow waters, it slows down. By the time it reaches shore, it is traveling at about 50 kilo-meters (30 miles) per hour. But now the waves have formed a huge wall of water—up to 30 meters (100 feet) high.

> * It's a Fact! *
> Not all underwater earthquakes produce tsunamis. The quake must be powerful—usually higher than magnitude 6.8—to cause a tsunami.

Not all tsunamis are destructive. In some cases, the waves are no worse than a fast-rising tidal wave, causing minor flood-ing in low-lying coastal areas. But some tsunamis may form a towering wall of water called a bore. Once they hit land, they may move many miles inland and flood villages and towns on the way. The crashing waves can rip trees out of the ground, destroy entire houses, and sweep people and animals away.

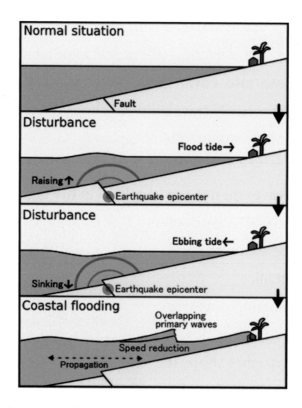

This illustration shows how the sea level rises the closer a tsunami gets to shore. As the sea level rises, however, the speed of the tsunami slows.

Soon the waves flow back out to the ocean, dragging everything along with them.

Usually there are multiple tsunamis. After ten to sixty minutes or so, just when people think the danger is over, another tsunami arrives. The first wave is not always the most destructive one. The second or third may be even more violent than the one before.

Tsunami Warnings

After 2004's huge tsunami disaster, people argued that many lives could have been saved if there had been an effective warning system in the Indian Ocean. At that time, the United States had two tsunami warning systems set up, one in the Pacific Ocean near Hawaii and another in the Pacific near Alaska, Canada, and the West Coast of the United States. In June 2006, the Indian Ocean tsunami warning system was established.

Are Tsunamis the Same as Tidal Waves?

No. Although people sometimes call tsunamis tidal waves by mistake, they are *not* tidal waves. Tides occur regularly, usually twice a day. They are effects of gravity: the pull of the moon and the sun on the earth. These forces act on the ocean water. So the surface of the ocean rises and falls according to the positions of the sun, moon, and earth. Tsunamis are not caused by the tides, but are the result of other forces, such as earthquakes.

Tsunami warning centers keep track of earthquakes around the world. When scientists detect a strong earthquake near a body of water, they check the tide gauges in harbors in the area to see if a tsunami has formed. The tsunami centers then issue a warning to all at-risk areas. Tsunami warnings are very accurate—a warning means a tsunami *is* coming. People in the area must evacuate their homes and find safety on higher ground.

STAYING SAFE

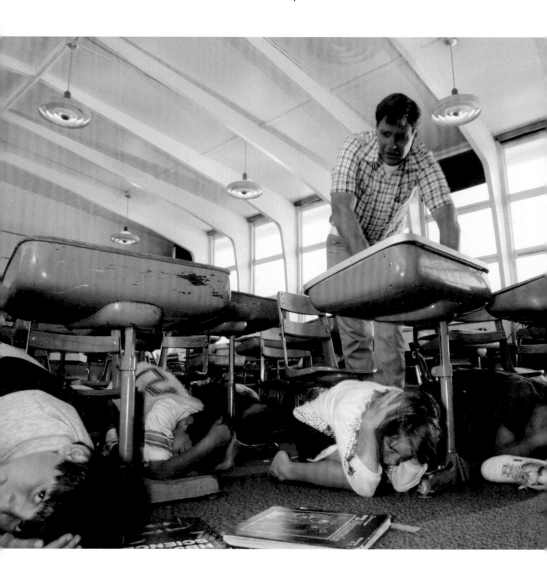

Millions of people all over

the world live in places where earthquakes and tsunamis are common. They must prepare for these natural disasters. In fact, they routinely practice earthquake safety in public schools and workplaces. That way people in high-risk areas will know what to do in case an earthquake or tsunami hits their area.

In Case of Emergency

If you live in an area where earthquakes and tsunamis are likely, there are some things you and your family can do to help you stay safe. It is important to have an emergency plan. There are probably special shelters in your area. Know where they are and the fastest way to get to them.

School children practice an earthquake drill in Parkfield, California. The building is earthquake resistant, with shatter-proof windows and a loud earthquake alarm.

Vacation Alert!

During the 2004 Indian Ocean tsunami, many people were on a holiday vacation in Thailand and other nearby regions when the tsunami hit on December 26. At the time, even residents were unprepared for such a disaster. But now people who live there realize it could happen again.

Whether you live in a high-risk area or are going on vacation to one, be prepared. Find out what to do in case of an earthquake or tsunami emergency.

Your school may have regular earthquake drills to practice what to do. Pay attention so you will remember if a real earthquake occurs.

At home, keep a kit with emergency supplies handy. It should include:

- Flashlight and batteries
- Battery-operated radio
- First aid kit
- Canned food and non-electric can opener
- Supply of water
- Special items for babies, the elderly, and pets
- Protective clothing and shoes
- Blankets

Falling objects can be a real danger during an earthquake. You can reduce your risk by earthquake-proofing your house.

- Keep all bookcases, china cabinets, and other tall furniture bolted to the wall so they won't fall over in an earthquake.

- Keep all heavy objects on the lower shelves. No objects, such as ceiling fans, should be hanging over beds.
- Cabinets should have strong latches to keep them closed.
- Hot water heaters should be strapped to the wall.

Earthquakes come without warning. But after an earthquake, many people can be saved by listening for tsunami warnings on the radio or TV. If you live in a high-risk tsunami area, follow the instructions. If the local officials say to go to higher ground, don't waste time. Leave as quickly as you can. Don't be curious and watch the waves up close. Many people are killed by tsunamis because of curiosity. That's what happened during the 2004 Indian Ocean tsunami.

When the Shaking Begins

If the ground beneath you starts to shake, remember a few key words: DROP, COVER, and HOLD ON. If you are in a house or building, duck or drop to the floor. Take cover under a sturdy table, desk, or other furniture. Hold on to it and be ready to move with it if you have to. Stay where you are until the ground stops shaking.

Do not leave the house. You could be hit by falling objects outside, such as street signs and pieces from buildings. Inside the house, stay away from windows, woodstoves, and any heavy furniture or appliances that might fall on you.

In an Earthquake, Is It Safer to Be on the Lower or Upper Level of a House or Building?

It is safer to be on the upper level of a house or building. In a strong earthquake, the building structure may crumble. If you are on the bottom floor, you could be crushed by the upper levels. You have a better chance of surviving by riding it out upstairs.

If you are outside when the earthquake hits, find an open area, away from any buildings or power lines. If you are in a car, the driver should move the car to a safe area. Stay away from bridges, tunnels, and overpasses. If possible, do not park under trees, light posts, signs, or power lines. In the mountains, be aware of any falling rock or snow that might have been loosened by the earthquake. At the beach, move quickly to higher ground or several hundred yards (meters) inland.

When the shaking finally stops, be aware of aftershocks that may follow.

Earthquake-Proof Buildings?

We cannot prevent earthquakes, but we can lessen the damage that they cause. Engineers have been studying what happens during an earthquake and working on designs for buildings, bridges, and highway overpasses that will be able to handle the tremendous forces involved.

The building Taipei 101 stands in Taipei, Taiwan, with 101 floors above ground and five floors below ground. It was built to be earthquake-proof.

Developing stronger building materials can help. Buildings with brick and concrete-block walls suffer the most damage in an earthquake. These building materials are just stacked one on top of another. They form solid walls that can hold up the weight of upper levels and roofs. But the sideways movements of an earthquake can shake them apart. And then the roof can fall in.

> *** It's a Fact! ***
> Many buildings in the poorer countries of the world are built from weak materials such as concrete blocks. That is the main reason why earthquakes in those areas bring huge numbers of deaths.

A sturdy framework made of stronger materials, such as steel, helps to hold buildings up during an earthquake. This is especially important for tall office buildings and high-rise apartments. Some modern buildings are made with a flexible support between the building and its foundation. If an earthquake shakes the foundation sideways, the support moves the opposite way. The building sways but does not collapse.

Even the new designs and ultra-strong materials cannot make buildings completely earthquake-proof. But they can save lives.

What if the "big one" does hit sometime in the future? Are we ready? Whether it is the "big one" or some other powerful earthquake, damage and destruction are unavoidable. People who choose to live in high-risk areas need to be prepared and learn how to live there safely.

CHAPTER NOTES

CHAPTER 1. WORLD SERIES EARTHQUAKE

1. "The Quake Hits During the World Series," *Exploratorium: Faultline*, 1999, video provided by KGO-TV News/ABC-7 News, <http://www.exploratorium.edu/faultline/activezone/media/vid-worldseries.html> (July 21, 2008).

2. Carl W. Stover and Jerry L. Coffman, "Historic Earthquakes: Santa Cruz Mountains (Loma Prieta), California 1989 10 18 00:04:15 UTC (Local 1989 10 17 05:04:15 p.m. PDT) Magnitude 6.9, Intensity IX," *USGS Earthquake Hazards Program*, January 25, 2007, <http://earthquake.usgs.gov/regional/states/events/1989_10_18.php> (October 12, 2007).

3. Edited by Roger D. Borcherdt, "The Loma Prieta, California, Earthquake of October 17, 1989—Strong Ground Motion," *U.S. Geological Survey*, 1994, <http://pubs.usgs.gov/pp/pp1551/pp1551a/> (October 30, 2007).

4. Elizabeth M. Colvard and James Rogers, "Facing the Great Disaster: How the Men and Women of the U.S. Geological Survey Responded to the 1906 'San Francisco Earthquake,'" *U.S. Geological Survey*, 2006, <http://pubs.usgs.gov/gip/2006/31/gip-31.pdf> (October 30, 2007).

CHAPTER 2. UNDERSTANDING EARTHQUAKES

1. U.S. Geological Survey, "FAQ — Historic Earthquakes and Earthquake Statistics," *Earthquake Hazards Program*, February 23, 2007, <http://earthquake.usgs.gov/learning/faq.php?categoryID=11&faqID=95> (November 2, 2007).

2. Ibid.

CHAPTER 3. WHEN THE EARTH SHAKES

1. Patrice A. Kohl, Ann P. O'Rourke, et al., "The Sumatran-Andaman Earthquake and Tsunami of 2004: The Hazards, Events, and Damages," *Prehospital and Disaster Medicine*, November–December 2005, p. 358, <http://pdm.medicine.wisc.edu/20-6%20PDFs/patrice.pdf> (July 29, 2008).

CHAPTER 4. THE DANGERS OF EARTHQUAKES

1. U.S. Geological Survey, "Earthquake Facts," *Earthquake Hazards Program*, September 7, 2007, <http://earthquake.usgs.gov/learning/facts.php> (November 15, 2007).

2. Ibid.

CHAPTER 5. TSUNAMIS

1. U.S. Geological Survey, "Fewer Deaths than 2004, but Earthquakes Still Kill Nearly 90,000 in 2005," *USGS Release*, January 12, 2006, <http://www.usgs.gov/newsroom/article.asp?ID=1428> (November 27, 2007).

GLOSSARY

aftershocks Tremors that follow a large earthquake.

avalanche (A-vuh-LANCH) The falling or sliding of large amounts of snow downhill at tremendous speeds.

body waves Faster seismic waves that move through the earth.

bore A fast-rising wall of water moving inland.

continents The large landmasses.

convergent (con-VER-gent) **boundaries** Boundaries between tectonic plates that are moving toward each other.

core The innermost part of the earth.

crust The outermost (surface) layer of the earth.

divergent (die-VER-gent) **boundaries** Boundaries between tectonic plates that are moving apart.

earthquake A trembling or shaking of the ground due to vibrations in the earth's crust caused by sudden movements of tectonic plates.

earthquake belt A long area of frequent earthquake activity.

epicenter (EP-i-SEN-ter) The spot on the surface directly above an earthquake's focus.

fault A crack in the earth's surface; the boundary between moving tectonic plates.

focus The place where rocks break or move, producing an earthquake.

foreshocks Small tremors that occur before a large earthquake.

friction The force generated by the motion of one object moving over another.

landslide The falling or sliding of large amounts of soil and rocks downhill at tremendous speeds.

liquefaction (LIK-wuh-FAK-shun) The process of turning soil and sand into a fluid-like substance during an earthquake.

Love wave A faster type of surface wave that moves the ground from side to side as it travels through the earth's surface.

magma Hot, melted rock beneath or within the earth's crust.

mantle The layer of the earth between the crust and the core.

plate boundaries The edges of the tectonic plates.

P waves (primary waves) The fastest body waves, which stretch and squeeze rocks in the earth's crust.

Rayleigh wave A slower type of surface wave that rolls along the earth's surface like waves on the ocean.

Ring of Fire A region along the edges of the Pacific Ocean, in which volcanoes and earthquakes are common.

S waves (secondary waves) Slower body waves that produce a shearing movement, up and down or sideways.

seismic (SIZE-mik) **waves** Vibrations transmitted through the earth during an earthquake.

seismograph (SIZE-moe-GRAF) An instrument that measures the vibrations transmitted through the earth during an earthquake. The recording is called a **seismogram.**

seismologist (SIZE-MOLL-o-jist) A scientist who detects, measures, and studies earthquakes.

strike-slip fault a transform boundary between two tectonic plates sliding past each other.

subduction (sub-DUK-shun) A process at the boundary of two colliding tectonic plates in which one plate is drawn down under or overridden by the other.

surface waves Slower seismic waves that move along the earth's surface.

tectonic (tek-TAH-nik) **plates** The large pieces of rock that make up the earth's crust.

tiltmeter (TILT-MEE-ter) An instrument that measures changes in the angle of the Earth's surface.

transform boundaries Boundaries between tectonic plates that slide past each other.

tremor A shaking movement; a vibration.

trench A long, narrow tunnel in the sea floor, where subduction occurs.

tsunami (tsoo-NAH-mee *or* soo-NAH-mee) An unusually large ocean wave produced by an earthquake or undersea volcanic eruption.

volcano A cone-shaped mountain formed by lava and ash around an opening in the earth's crust through which hot matter from the mantle erupts.

FURTHER READING AND INTERNET ADDRESSES

Adamson, Thomas K. *Tsunamis*. Mankato, Minn.: Capstone Press, 2006.

Green, Jen. *Understanding Volcanoes and Earthquakes*. New York: Powerkids Press, 2008.

Steele, Philip and Neil Morris. *Inside Earthquakes*. Strongsville, Ohio: Gareth Stevens Publishing, 2006.

Stewart, Melissa. *Earthquakes and Volcanoes FYI*. New York: HarperCollins, 2008.

National Geographic Kids: Earthquake!

<http://www.nationalgeographic.com/ngkids/0403/>

Animation with facts and photos about earthquakes and the damage they cause; video of a San Francisco neighborhood hit by an earthquake.

National Oceanic and Atmospheric Administration (NOAA): "Tsunami Information for Kids"

<http://www.tsunami.noaa.gov/kids.html>

Includes a tsunami warning brochure for kids, a tsunami trivia quiz, and links to other tsunami sites.

U.S. Geological Survey: "Earthquakes for Kids"

<http://earthquake.usgs.gov/learning/kids/>

Find out what earthquakes have occurred in the past week and month, and about important earthquakes in history; other pages include Cool Earthquake Facts, Earthquake Pictures, The Science of Earthquakes, Science Fair Project Ideas, Puzzles and Games, and Become an Earthquake Scientist.

INDEX